EXTINCT

EXTINCT

TRILOBITE

Ben Garrod

Illustrated by Gabriel Ugueto

ZEPHYR

An imprint of Head of Zeus

Head of Zeus Ltd
5–8 Hardwick Street
London EC1R 4RG
WWW.HEADOFZEUS.COM

'Now I am become Death, the destroyer of worlds.'

The Bhagavad-Gita

CONTENTS

INTRODUCTION

For as long as there has been life on Earth, there has been extinction, and given enough time, all species will one day go extinct. It is all too easy to think extinction is terrible and that we should do all we can to stop a species from going extinct. That makes complete sense, doesn't it? Right now, around one million species of plants, animals and other organisms are at real risk of going extinct because of our actions and we should do all we can to save as many of these wonderful species as possible.

But as bad and as sad as some extinctions are, the process of extinction itself is a natural one, and it is something that helps drive evolution and the development of more species.

I'm an evolutionary biologist and I've worked with some of the strangest, most beautiful, iconic and heartbreakingly threatened animals on our planet, from majestic tiger sharks and beautiful walruses to our own closest living relatives, the chimpanzee. We talk about extinction a lot but how much do you *really* know about it?

I wanted to write this series to explain what's at stake if we carry on pushing so many other species into extinction. I want to explore extinction as a biological process and investigate why it can sometimes be a positive thing for evolution, as well as, at times, nature's most destructive force. Let's put it under the microscope and find out everything there is to know about it. Extinction is an incredible process and understanding it enables us to understand the world that little bit better and to make a difference.

When a species goes extinct, we place a dagger symbol (†) next to its name when it's listed or mentioned in a scientific manner. So, if you do see the name of a species with a little dagger after it, you'll know why. It's extinct. In this series, I have written about eight fantastic species.

Starting with *Hallucigenia* (†), then *Dunkleosteus* (†) and trilobites (†), through to *Lisowicia* (†), *Tyrannosaurus rex* (†) and megalodon (†), before finishing on thylacine (†) and lastly, the Hainan gibbon. Of these, only the Hainan gibbon does not have a dagger next to its scientific name, meaning it is the only one we still have a chance of saving from extinction.

Professor Ben Garrod

WHAT IS EXTINCTION?

THERE ARE LOTS of forces and processes in nature. Some make us think of positive things, such as birth and growth; some are neutral, such as photosynthesis and seasons; and others make us think negative things. Death and extinction are definitely on that last list. But species evolve – they change and adapt to their environments and eventually, they go extinct. It's all a part of the natural life cycle of every species. The problem with extinction is that some are natural and are to be expected, while others are because of us and can (and should) be stopped.

Before investigating when we should try to tackle extinction, we first need to understand it as a natural process. What drives extinction, and what makes some species go extinct more easily than others? When we hear the words 'extinct' or 'extinction', we usually think two things. First, we always seem to imagine the same few species. I bet you thought of a dodo, a mammoth and probably a dinosaur, maybe *Tyrannosaurus rex*? Second, you might be forgiven for thinking that an extinct animal almost deserved it somehow. Maybe they weren't quite as well adapted as they could be or they simply didn't try hard enough.

Well, both ideas are wrong. First, dinosaurs and dodos aren't the only animals to have gone extinct. And second, as I've already mentioned, going extinct is natural and happens to pretty much every type of animal, plant, fungi, bacteria and other life form that has ever existed or is ever likely to, and has nothing to do with how 'good' or 'bad' a species is.

Even a quick look at extinction shows us how widespread, devastating and yet important it is. But before we understand all that, what exactly do we mean by the word extinct? We may have a general idea that it's something to do with a species not being 'alive' anymore. Something is extinct when the last individual of that species or group dies and there are absolutely no more to replace it. Because extinction has been present since the first life on Earth popped into existence, this must mean that loads and loads of species have gone extinct.

It's hard to get your head around how many species this has happened to already. Scientists predict that as many as 99 per cent of the species that have *ever* lived have gone extinct and if you're wondering how many species that might actually be, then, if their calculations are correct, it means we have already lost an almost unbelievable five billion species from our planet.

It's nearly impossible to be certain because many of these extinctions stretch back millions (or even hundreds of millions) of years and, because there wasn't a scientist standing there with a camera or a notebook, we shall never know about many of these species. Even today, scientists believe that there may be 10–14 million different species (although some scientists think this figure might even be as high as one trillion) but of those, only 1.2 million have been documented and recorded in a proper scientific way. This means that we don't know about 90 per cent of life on planet Earth right now.

Here's where it gets a little complicated. Extinction is natural. Even we human beings will go extinct one day. It might sound sad but that's because you're thinking from the point of view of a person. We are simply one of those 14 million or so species, remember. Usually, a species has about 10 million years or so of evolving, eating, chasing, playing, maybe doing homework, building nests or even going to the moon before it goes extinct and ends up in the history (or even prehistory) books. Some species last longer than this, some are around for less time.

Every single species evolves to be perfectly suited to a particular ecosystem or habitat and acts in a way that will help it survive and have young. We call this its *niche*. Extinction happens when a species can no longer survive in its niche. Lots of different things can cause this and some are more natural than others. Some kill off one species and others cause the loss of thousands or even millions of species at once, making extinction one of the most complex, interesting and important things to study in science.

WHY DO SPECIES GO EXTINCT?

A RECENT report stated that approximately one million (1,000,000) species on Earth are threatened with extinction. This number already sounds unthinkably high, but it only includes animals and plants and not any of the other groups of living organisms essential to the well-being of the planet. If they were included, then the number would be even higher. Much higher.

But why *do* species go extinct? It's not as though human hunters will kill all these species and realistically, climate change can't be responsible for every single loss. As you'll see, there are lots of reasons for extinction, but is there a common link? What makes certain species more likely to go extinct than others? It's an interesting question, which many scientists are investigating.

At its most simple, extinction occurs when something bad happens too quickly in the environment of a species or is too severe for the species to overcome. Imagine if a large flightless member of the pigeon family lived on an island in the middle of a tropical ocean. Think what would happen if explorers and sailors stopped there. What if they then accidentally introduced pest species – such as rats, which ate the birds' eggs – as well as goats and pigs for themselves to eat, and these mammals competed with the big flightless birds for food. With the birds being hunted, their nests being raided and having to compete with new mammals for food, there was only one place for this species to go... into the history books. If this imaginary scenario sounds familiar, then maybe you're thinking of the dodo and what led to the extinction of one of the most iconic species on the planet.

When a species does not have the opportunity to respond to a change in the environment, then it is likely to go extinct. What sort of response do I mean here? Well, it might be a physical change, such as colour or shape, or a change that's seen only at the genetic level, such as better resistance to a particular disease. It might even be a change in behaviour, such as being active at a different time of the day or an alteration in migration patterns.

And in terms of what sort of 'changes in the environment' might cause an extinction, these can be in the physical environment of the species, such as the actual destruction of a habitat, flooding or drought. Or the change might be in its 'biological environment', such as the arrival of a new predator or the development of a new deadly disease. For each of these, if the species does not adapt, then it will die out and become extinct.

Scientists have estimated that the average 'lifespan' of a species is between one million and 10 million years, before it goes extinct. Some will last longer and others for only a fraction of that time. There are a variety of causes that can contribute directly or indirectly to the extinction of a species or group of species:

DISEASES, PREDATION AND COMPETITION

Sometimes, extinctions can be caused by organisms so small they cannot be seen without the most powerful microscopes. When sailors turned up on Christmas Island in the Indian Ocean hundreds of years ago, they took all sorts of things with them in their ships. They had food and drink to last long voyages, navigation equipment with which to explore and map the world, and eventually the building supplies they needed to settle on the island and make homes. They also accidentally took other things, like black rats, which were stowaways on the ships.

When these rats made it ashore, they took their diseases with them. But when they met the rats that lived on the island, suddenly the island rats

were introduced
to diseases from
which they had no
immunity. The black
rats carried parasites, which
infected the local Christmas Island
rats when fleas jumped from one rat to
another. Over the next several hundred years, the
disease took its toll and, as far as we know, the last
Christmas Island rat died in 1903, making the
species extinct.

In a natural situation, it's very unusual for a predator to cause the total extinction of its prey, because the two are in balance, where each evolves to be a better predator or to be better at avoiding predators. This delicate relationship takes millions of years and is a good example of what we call coevolution, where the evolution of two species is closely tied together. But when a predator is suddenly introduced to an environment, then the prey has no time to evolve in order to avoid being eaten. Flightless birds can't suddenly fly or brightly coloured fish can't suddenly develop camouflage to avoid new predators that are introduced into their environments.

When Europeans introduced cats and foxes into Australia, many of the country's native animals had no defence against them. One of these unfortunate species was the southern pig-footed bandicoot, a small marsupial with unusual hoof-like feet. In the 1950s, as little as 150 years after the introduction of the predators, the pig-footed bandicoot went extinct.

Making sure you don't run out of food is a pretty essential part of the plan for any long trip. When sailors explored the world hundreds of years ago, they'd drop off goats on newly discovered islands, so the goats would breed and there'd be a ready supply of food when the sailors next stopped by. One place where this happened was on the Galápagos Islands in the Pacific Ocean. It seemed like the perfect idea... apart from the fact that there were already hundreds of thousands of similar-sized herbivores on the islands. But whereas the goats were fast moving and able to climb almost anywhere, the original inhabitants – giant tortoises – were much slower and weren't quite as good at getting to those hard-to-reach places.

Before long, the goats bred and bred and were everywhere. The tortoises, on the other hand, were not able to compete and their numbers dropped, from tens of thousands to a few thousand survivors. Before these unique tortoises went extinct, action was taken and it was decided to remove nearly 250,000 goats from the islands. Luckily, the tortoise population is now recovering, which is great news, but because the population is still only around 10 per cent of what it was before the goats were introduced, there is still a long way to go.

When goats were introduced across the Galápagos Islands by humans for food, they very nearly led to the extinction of the islands' famous giant tortoises.

COEXTINCTION

Sometimes, a species has evolved alongside another species so closely that when one goes extinct, there is nothing the other can do but go extinct too. This might be a specific parasite depending on a specific host species or maybe a particular pollinating insect needing one species of plant in order to survive. One extreme example of a coextinction is the moa and the Haast's eagle. Moa were huge flightless birds found on New Zealand, with some being as much as 3.6m in height and 230kg in weight. The Haast's eagle was their main predator. When human settlers hunted the last moa into extinction around 600 years ago, the eagles were left with no food and they too went extinct.

GENETIC MIXING

Every species has its own set of genetic data unique to that particular species. It's like the recipe for the species. If any bit of it is changed, then it's a different species, just like a recipe. (Imagine trying to make a chocolate cake but mixing up that recipe with another one for bangers and mash – that would be weird, right?) When the genetic material for a species is altered by the presence of 'other' genetic material, we call this 'genetic mixing'. This can happen naturally or because humans are to blame.

As well as happening between species, this genetic mixing can occur within a species. You may never have noticed, but there is more than one species of zebra. In fact, there are three. The plains zebra is fairly common, the mountain zebra less so, and the Grévy's zebra is much rarer and is classed as being endangered. Its numbers have dropped from around 15,000 to just 2,400 in the last 50 years. Human hunting, diseases from cattle and other livestock, and habitat destruction and loss are the main reasons for its decline. Some conservation groups say this is among the most worrying reductions of range of any African mammal.

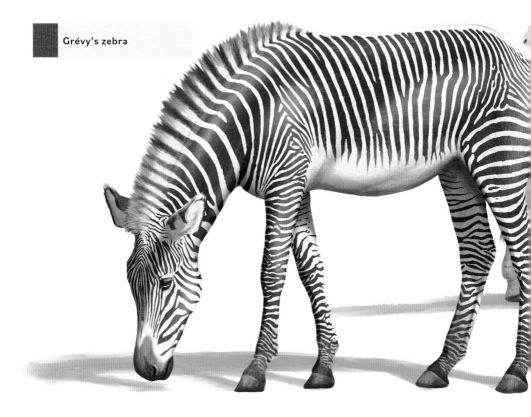

Grévy's zebra

Another problem, however, is that male plains zebras have mated with female Grévy's zebras, producing offspring that are a mixture of the two species. If this carries on, it's possible that there will no longer be any pure-bred Grévy's zebras. Eventually, we would be left with the plains zebra and the mountain zebra, but also a new species, formed from the mixing of the plains and Grévy's zebras.

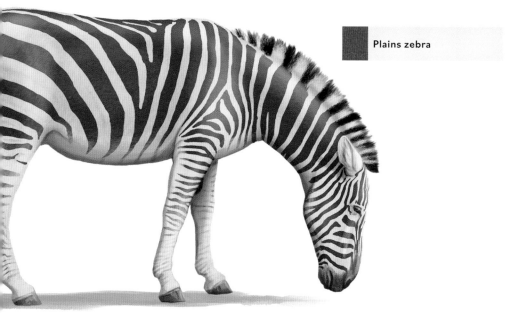

Plains zebra

HABITAT DESTRUCTION

It's clear to see how habitat destruction (and change) is causing extinctions now, but there is evidence in the fossil record, and from looking at the geological record, that the loss of crucial habitats has been responsible for species extinctions for hundreds of millions of years. It's a problem that has largely led to the million or so species being threatened with extinction right now.

Sometimes, however, it is possible to recover from what seems like an impossible situation. The very small but brightly coloured ladybird spider is found across parts of western Europe. Destruction of its heathland habitat led this iconic red, black and white arachnid almost to go extinct in the 1980s. In the UK, just seven individuals were left at one point, but through habitat restoration and other amazing conservation work, they are now back up to a healthy population. They're the perfect example of a real success story and why it's never too late to try to make a difference in conservation.

CLIMATE CHANGE

We hear a lot about how climate change leads to many extinctions now, but, like habitat destruction, it has been a leading cause of species disappearing for millions of years. If you were able to peer back in time just a few million years, Earth might appear similar but the animals would look very different. In Africa, for example, there was a whole collection of mammals which have now completely disappeared. There were giant baboons the size of gorillas, huge relatives of modern-day elephants called *Deinotherium* (DI-NO thir-EE-um), which probably weighed twice as much as elephants and had backward-curving tusks, and the unusual-looking *Sivatherium* (SEE-va thir-EE-um), which was a 3m-tall relative of the giraffe, with two  sets of antler-like structures. All roamed across Africa. These mammals, and many more, died out over four and a half million years ago. For many years, scientists believed our early human ancestors were to blame, but more recent research has shown that naturally occurring climate change was responsible for the extinction of these prehistoric mammals.

Even fairly recently, places many of us are familiar with now would have seemed very different. Just a few million years ago, western Europe would have been home to rhinos, chalicotheres, which are extinct members of the group that includes horses and rhinos, and huge relatives of modern-day elephants called *Deinotherium*.

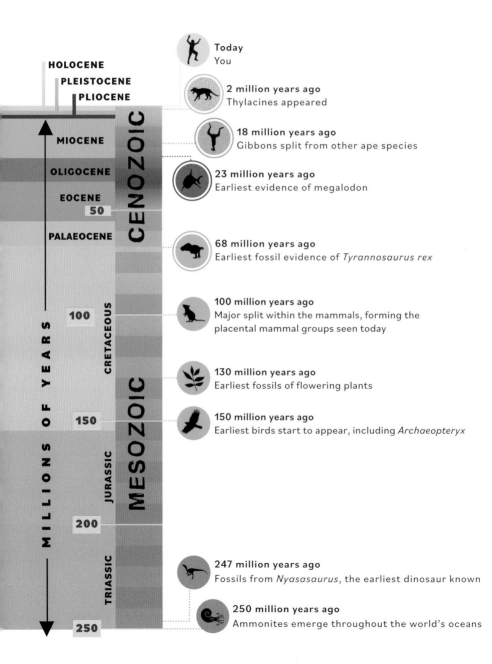

HOLOCENE
PLEISTOCENE
PLIOCENE

Today
You

2 million years ago
Thylacines appeared

18 million years ago
Gibbons split from other ape species

23 million years ago
Earliest evidence of megalodon

68 million years ago
Earliest fossil evidence of *Tyrannosaurus rex*

100 million years ago
Major split within the mammals, forming the placental mammal groups seen today

130 million years ago
Earliest fossils of flowering plants

150 million years ago
Earliest birds start to appear, including *Archaeopteryx*

247 million years ago
Fossils from *Nyasasaurus*, the earliest dinosaur known

250 million years ago
Ammonites emerge throughout the world's oceans

CENOZOIC

MIOCENE
OLIGOCENE
EOCENE
50
PALAEOCENE

MESOZOIC

CRETACEOUS
100
150

JURASSIC
200

TRIASSIC
250

MILLIONS OF YEARS

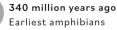

MILLIONS OF YEARS

PERMIAN

300

CARBONIFEROUS

350

DEVONIAN

400

SILURIAN

450

ORDOVICIAN

500

CAMBRIAN

PALAEOZOIC

PROTEROZOIC

ARCHEAN

300 million years ago
Lisowicia first appeared

320 million years ago
'Mammal-like reptiles', including *Dimetrodon*, evolve

340 million years ago
Earliest amphibians

382 million years ago
Earliest evidence of *Dunkleosteus*

385 million years ago
Oldest fossilised tree

400 million years ago
Earliest fossils of insects

Some of the dates for earliest fossils are estimates based on our best understanding right now. They are not always perfect and the more evidence we collect, the more certain we can be and the more accurate these dates will eventually become.

500 million years ago
Fossil evidence from *Hallucigenia*

520 million years ago
Earliest vertebrates emerged (and may have looked like small eels)

530 million years ago
Earliest fossils of trilobites

680 million years ago
Earliest ancestors of jellyfish and their relatives

2.15 billion years ago
Earliest evidence of bacteria

3 billion years ago
Earliest evidence of viruses

MASS EXTINCTIONS

RIGHT NOW, somewhere in the world, something, for some reason, will be going extinct, hopefully due to natural causes. In the same way that the evolution and appearance of a species is completely natural, so too is the constant loss of species. Species come and go in a constant cycle, a little bit like the tides moving back and forth or the changing of the seasons.

Extinction is unavoidable and goes on at a fairly predictable rate wherever life exists. We call this background extinction: constant, low-level extinction which doesn't really cause major problems on a wider scale – other than for the species going extinct, that is. These 'everyday extinctions' go mostly unnoticed by the majority of us.

This all changes when we talk about a mass extinction. Mass extinctions, as you might expect, involve loss of life on a huge scale, either across a large number of species or groups, or across a significant part of the planet, or both. In a mass extinction event, the rate of species being lost is greater than the rate by which species are evolving. Imagine you're slowly filling a bucket with water but there's a big hole in its side; over time, that bucket will still become empty.

Over the last 500 million years or so, the Earth has experienced multiple mass extinctions, ranging from five to as many as 20 (depending on what definitions (and there are a number of different ones) scientists use). In the worst of these mass extinction events, over 90 per cent of life on Earth has been wiped out, and in terms of life recovering to a level from before the event, it may take at least 10 million years for biodiversity levels to return to what they were. Some mass extinctions, like the one caused by the asteroid 66 million years ago at the end of the Cretaceous period, are pretty quick, while others spread across hundreds of thousands of years to take full effect.

When we talk about mass extinctions, most scientists agree there are five classic mass extinctions, with the earliest occurring around 450 million years ago and the most recent 66 million years ago. In addition to these famous five mass extinctions, another was identified recently, which struck around 2.5 million years ago.

Now, many scientists say we are entering (or even in) the sixth mass extinction event, but this is something that needs to be looked at closely for two reasons. First, I've just mentioned the recently identified mass extinction that occurred just over two million years ago, which would make that the sixth mass extinction and the current global extinction event would be the seventh, in fact. Second, as we'll see later in the series, it's really hard to say exactly when most mass extinctions start, so, as bad as it is right now, we may not even be in one yet.

Throughout the series, we're going to look at the five classic mass extinctions, the newly discovered mass extinction and the current extinction event, which is being triggered by us. Finally, we'll look at how scientists and conservationists are tackling the threat of extinction now and explore what can be done.

THE PERMIAN MASS EXTINCTION

IF YOU COMBINED every disaster movie ever made, it wouldn't be anywhere near as bad as what happened to our planet 252 million years ago. Gigantic patches of land were covered in flowing lava for tens of thousands of years, and habitats so cold they'd freeze your blood were next to environments so hot that many animals cooked alive. There were oceans choked with deadly chemicals, huge explosions and fireballs, burning acid rain and, in places, not enough oxygen to breathe. If a film *was* made featuring this many disasters, you'd be forgiven for thinking it wasn't believable. But, a quarter of a billion years ago, it *did* happen. And it all happened simultaneously. Life itself was very nearly made extinct.

The End Permian (pur-ME-an) mass extinction was the closest we've come to completely losing all life, when as much as 97 per cent of Earth's marine species and 75 per cent of land-living animals died – in fact, it is sometimes known as the Great Dying. The only reason you are here now reading this book is because you are descended from one of those very, very lucky few survivors from over a quarter of a billion years ago.

After the previous mass extinction in the Late Devonian (dev-O NEE-an), which lasted for around 20 million years and ended 359 million years ago, the Earth started to recover. Once again, life extended through the oceans and also across the land more extensively. The Devonian saw the end of 'the Age of the Fishes', and the planet entered the Carboniferous (car-bon if-ferr-us), which lasted for around 60 million years. Following this came the Permian period, which started 298.9 million years ago and lasted for a little over 46 million years. The Permian was split into three smaller sections, or epochs (EE-poks), and the End Permian mass extinction marked the end of this time frame, about 252.2 million years ago.

CAUSES 🌡️❄️

As with any mystery thriller, there are always lots of clues and theories as to who the culprit might be, and the same is true for the greatest extinction event in the Earth's history. One idea put forward is that there was a giant asteroid strike, which wiped out almost everything. It's a great idea and if it was true for one mass extinction, then maybe it could be used to explain another one too.

But as ever with science, we have to look at the evidence and when we look for tell-tale signs of an extra-terrestrial asteroid strike, there is nothing to suggest this was to blame. First, there was no impact site, as there was with the later 'dinosaur-killing' extinction, and looking closer, there was no fine layer of iridium (irr-id EE-um), one of the rarest and densest elements on the planet. Iridium was brought from space on the asteroid which marked the end of the more recent Cretaceous period, and because the impact was so great, a thin line of it was left around much of the planet.

When scientists looked even more closely at what was going on towards the end of the Permian, they saw that even before the mass extinction, things were already troublesome. There had been a series of smaller extinctions,

such as Olson's extinction, 20 million years earlier. This claimed *Dimetrodon* (dim-et RO don), among others.

Think about a volcano and what a volcanic eruption looks like... a big towering cone, like an upturned funnel, spewing lava and with red-hot streams flowing down its sides. Although this might describe the classic idea of volcanic activity, it does not even begin to describe what happened at the end of the Permian period. Instead, there was a vast area of lava, called a lava field. This immense area of fiery landscape was caused by changes and movement of the huge tectonic plates which sit within the Earth's crust. It is known as the Siberian Traps and remains the largest and most widespread lava field in history.

The giant lava field burned for nearly two million years and, in that time, almost four million square kilometres was covered by lava, ranging in depth from between 400m and an unimaginable 3km. There was so much lava that it could have covered the entire USA in a layer a kilometre deep. You'd be right in thinking that this much lava would have devastating effects for any habitat or individual organism nearby, but its other wide-ranging impacts ultimately led to the largest of all the mass extinctions.

It's difficult to imagine just how inhospitable, lifeless and destructive the Siberian Traps would have been. Luckily, there is nothing like this environment on our planet today.

EFFECTS 🌞

We often think of things as simple contrasts, where we look at two extremes. Opposite sides of a coin, for example; up or down; good or bad; left or right; night or day. But nature doesn't work like that and from a scientific point of view, even night and day can be quite hard to separate. I've been lucky enough to spend a bit of time in the Arctic, right up towards the North Pole, where for weeks on end the sun never actually sets, even in the middle of the night.

But, despite saying nature isn't usually a case of extremes, the End Permian mass extinction was among the most extreme periods in Earth's history. One moment, life was thriving in and out of the vast oceans, with plants, animals and other groups of organisms busily evolving, and then '*wham*' – a series of events led to the loss of around 90 per cent of life on our planet. They were gone. Dead.

Extinctions within the end of the Permian period were often so sudden, there was no time for species to adapt and evolve. Instead, their evolutionary journey was erased forever. This was definitely, without question, an extreme event, with little warning or time to prepare. If the start of the Permian represents the day, then the end of the Permian period was the night, plunging life into darkness.

Life during the Permian was very different to what it had been in the Devonian period, before the previous mass extinction. On land, trees and a whole host of plant and animal life had started to boom into existence and diversify into different groups and individual species. The terrestrial fauna was dominated by a group of animals (now extinct) which had evolved from early Devonian fish and had managed to crawl on to the land. While one land-living group split off and became the reptiles, another, similar group developed into what looked like some sort of laboratory experiment gone wrong – where animals that were not quite reptiles, but not exactly mammals either, dominated the Permian landscape. More about them later.

The End Permian mass extinction ended not only the Permian period but it was so extreme, it also ended a larger block of time called the Palaeozoic (PAY-LEE O zo-ik) era. This era had covered the Cambrian, Ordovician, Silurian, Devonian, Carboniferous and Permian periods. Life in the Palaeozoic was so different to what would follow, the planet's biodiversity would never look the same again.

If the immediate effects of the largest lava field weren't bad enough, then another massive problem was the huge amount of gas released by all this volcanic activity. The worst of these gases was carbon dioxide, which caused rapid climate change, destroying ocean ecosystems across the planet.

The Siberian Traps would have been a major problem anywhere, but imagine if it had happened in places where there were vast amounts of coal and natural gas buried beneath the land. If you're thinking 'so what?', then remember that we burn coal and gas. Both are flammable. And to stick millions of tonnes of burning lava on top of millions of tonnes of flammable fossil fuels would be the worst idea. It would have caused massive explosions and unimaginably large fires.

Well, you guessed it, this is exactly what happened. Some of the largest deposits of coal and natural gas, sometimes over a kilometre thick in places, lay directly beneath where the Siberian Traps opened up. It's as though our prehistoric world really wanted to make sure the End Permian finished with a bang. So many enormous explosions and fires would have released high levels of another gas, methane, into the atmosphere, and this breaks down into carbon dioxide, so worsening the effects on climate change.

Scientists today are constantly worried about the levels of carbon dioxide being released into the atmosphere and it's important we measure and monitor the volume to gauge changes. At the moment, we estimate that around 40 gigatonnes of carbon dioxide is released into our atmosphere every year. It's hard to imagine how much this really is, but a single gigatonne is the same as a trillion kilograms, about the weight of a trillion bags of sugar!

When we look at the rate of carbon dioxide being released now, we can see that it's the fastest since before the End Permian mass extinction. We are well on our way to burning through all the fossil fuels on and in our planet, where as much as 5,000 gigatonnes of carbon dioxide might be released. This would change the face of our world, but far more was released 252.2 million years ago, when somewhere between 10,000 and 50,000 gigatonnes was added to our atmosphere.

A major effect of all this carbon dioxide was an increase in the temperature around the planet. Although you might not think it, the *average* temperature on Earth now is around 15°C, but at the end of the Permian period, our planet baked in heatwaves of 60°C, while coastal marine habitats in the great Panthalassa may have been as high as 40°C, much warmer than any shallow marine habitats we have today.

It's even possible that the massive increase in these (and other) greenhouse gases might have wrecked the ozone layer, which would have let more damaging radiation from the sun hit our planet. Over time, this may have caused genetic mutations and even deadly sunburn in many organisms living across different habitats and environments.

We talk about too much carbon dioxide being a bad thing, but if we really want to appreciate the full effects of what happened 252 million years ago, then we need to understand what happens when a load of extra CO^2 is pumped into our atmosphere. Although there's a long list of impacts, there are two most relevant and devastating effects in terms of talking about mass extinctions. First, extra CO^2 causes the planet to warm up because it stops heat from the sun, which has hit the Earth, radiating back into space, *just* like a greenhouse does. Increasing the temperature like this affects everything, from which plants can grow in an area to when different species can breed.

The second effect of increasing carbon dioxide levels is that it causes a major issue in the oceans and other marine ecosystems around the world. Carbon dioxide is absorbed by sea water, and the more there is, the more is absorbed. When these two ingredients react, they form an acid, called carbonic acid, which over time, will increase the acidity of the sea water itself. When this happens, it can damage huge parts of a marine ecosystem by killing small organisms which have either soft external skeletons, or shells that are destroyed by the acid.

In 2020, a group of scientists showed that one of the most important species of crab in the Pacific Ocean is in serious trouble because of an acid build-up. The Dungeness crab is eaten by millions of people and is part of the most valuable fisheries in North America, but their larvae are in trouble because higher levels of carbonic acid in the water

are killing them, causing the crab population to crash. As well as affecting the economy, this will have consequences for many other species within its environment. And that's just one species – imagine if thousands or even millions of species suddenly suffered in the same way. Scientists have shown that our oceans have increased in acidity by as much as 25 per cent in the last two hundred years or so. Looking ahead, and unless we take drastic action, this level is only set to increase further and further.

As scientists, we can't just talk about 'too much' or 'too little' of something, without knowing what the ideal levels are; so how much carbon dioxide *should* be in the atmosphere? We calculate this by looking at the ratio of a particular gas in relation to another and we use a unit called 'parts per million' (or ppm). If, for example, we look at the amount of krypton found in air (which is just one of the many gases that make up our atmosphere), we'd see that it represents a little bit over 1ppm. This means that the other 999,999 molecules within our sample of atmosphere would be from gases other than krypton.

If we look at the carbon dioxide in our atmosphere right now, it's 412ppm, which is already 50 per cent higher than it was 200 years ago. At this level, it is already causing devastating impacts for species around the world, but at the end of the Permian period, the level of carbon dioxide in the atmosphere was much higher, at around 4,000ppm, with some scientists believing it might even have been as much as a lethal 8,000ppm.

With huge parts of the supercontinent burning and toxic levels of carbon dioxide in the atmosphere, it became more and more difficult for life to survive and, stretching over 60,000 years, the End Permian mass extinction had enough time to kill off many groups.

More than 95 per cent of corals and sea anemones died out, as well as 97 per cent of marine slugs and snails. Only about 2 per cent of ammonites survived the mass extinction, but along with all the eurypterid (YOO-Rip tEr-idd) 'sea scorpions', 100 per cent of the trilobites (try-LO bite) finally went extinct.

At the end of the Permian, oceans around the world, which had previously been thriving, were left almost completely lifeless and dead.

Dr Anjana Khatwa is an Earth Scientist, specialising in bringing stories about the origins and formation of natural landscapes to life for a wide range of audiences. She lives in Dorset and spends her spare time filling her house with rocks and fossils that she finds on the Jurassic coast.

What on earth is a fossil?

Imagine walking along a beach, minding your own business and thinking of nothing in particular. Your eye stops on a smooth grey rock with strange markings on it. As you pick it up, your eyes sweep over the beautiful pattern on the surface and your fingers brush over the ridges that form a curious spiral shape. Congratulations! You are the first person to see the fossilised body of this ancient sea creature, an ammonite, that died almost 200 million years ago.

Fossils are the preserved remains of creatures, plants and processes that existed on Earth hundreds of millions of years ago. They are critical clues, often locked away in the rocks, that help us piece together the puzzle of what life was like on ancient Earth. But how do they form? Imagine our ammonite swimming about in a deep, murky Jurassic sea. When this animal died, it sank to the bottom of the seabed, and its soft body parts were either eaten by scavengers or rotted away. The hard shell that was left behind became buried under layers of silt and clay. As these soft layers of sediment built up, they transformed into hard rock layers and the enclosed shell was fossilised. The minerals in the shell were replaced by minerals in the surrounding rock, literally turning the shell into stone. Discovering fossils like these helps us to create a rich tapestry of what life on Earth used to be like.

In fact, the oldest fossils on Earth might be considered to be rather boring compared to the colossal dinosaur skeletons we are used to seeing. In 2017, scientists were astonished to discover that complex microbes extracted from sedimentary rocks collected in Western Australia dated back almost 3.5 billion years. It is truly amazing to think that these simple, yet diverse, micro-organisms would go on to evolve into more complex life and eventually humans. Over the course of Earth's history, fossils have helped us to analyse changes in climate, sea levels and, most critically, how life evolved and responded to these changing conditions.

But we must keep in mind that not everything can be fossilised. Soft tissue, eggs and even skin are exceptionally rare to find. Even trace fossils like footprints or sand ripples require a remarkable coincidence of nature which can bury the feature quickly in order to preserve its transient character.

It's this prospect of a chance find, an opportunity to turn over a rock and discover a secret that is new to science, that makes fossils and palaeontology one of the most exciting aspects of Earth Science.

TRILOBITE

IF I ASKED YOU to name some of the most successful groups of animals ever, which would you name? Maybe the sharks? They're brilliant predators, dominating so many marine ecosystem food chains. Or what about the dinosaurs? They were around for more than 150 million years, with examples such as *Spinosaurus*, *Patagotitan* and, of course, *Tyrannosaurus rex*. Or maybe mammals? With our own species part of this group, maybe we should be there with the best of the best?

Would you include trilobites in that list of ultimate animals? Probably not, I'm guessing. But in fact, the trilobites were one of the most successful groups of animals ever. Split into 10 different groups, there were more than an impressive 20,000 known species of trilobites across their 300 million years of existence. They were found in every marine habitat, from shallow coastal ecosystems to deep sea environments, and in both cold polar and warm tropical waters. First emerging some 530 million years ago, they thrived for over 300 million years before going extinct 252 million years ago in the End Permian mass extinction.

DISCOVERY 🔍

Being such a successful group means many people have known about trilobites for a long time. Sometimes, we know the exact date a fossil species was discovered and recognised for what it was, down to the year, place and person who made that discovery. This is the case with something like *Dunkleosteus* (*dun-kll osstee-us*), which was first discovered in the USA in 1867 by a man called Jay Terrell and his son. Other times, it's impossible to know who discovered something first. We have to be careful in science about saying someone discovered something for the first time, because often, people from local communities are already well aware of special species. For example, just because an unusual bird has never been filmed before doesn't mean it's never been seen by anyone. Local people might already use a tree as medicine, even though it is unknown to outsiders. Who knows who has seen fossils that are millions of years old? This appears to be the case with trilobites and once again, these amazing little marine invertebrates have a few surprises for us.

The first time a trilobite was scientifically described appears to have been by the Reverend Edward Lhwyd, who in 1698 wrote an article for one of the oldest scientific journals. He described some unusual 'stones' he'd found in Wales. One of them he described as a fish skeleton, but luckily for us, he also drew his findings, which show his stone fish skeleton was actually a fossilised trilobite. The name 'trilobite' was given to the group in the 19th century, 200 years later.

Trilobites were well known a long time before they were described as a stone fish skeleton in Wales, though. Some Native American communities wore ammonites as protective pendants, while the Greeks and Romans may also have prized them, calling them 'beetle stones'. In the late 19th century, archaeologists in France explored a cave and found stone spear tips and tools made from animal bones. Alongside them, they discovered a worn trilobite fossil in which someone had used a hand drill to create a little hole, maybe so they could wear it around their neck or hang within the cave. The artefacts within the cave turned out to be around 15,000 years old, meaning our early human ancestors must have thought   the little trilobite fossil important or special enough to drill the hole and keep it in the first place.

It appears we have been interested in trilobites for thousands of years but are only now revealing some of their most fascinating secrets.

ANATOMY

Sometimes we look at something but don't really *see* it. How often do you really count the number of wings on a fly or a bee? I'll give you a clue – they're different. Have you ever seen a close-up photo of a cat's tongue? How much does the plant on your windowsill move in one day? In science, the more we really look at something, the more we will be able to understand it. The same is true of the little trilobites. They are instantly recognisable, but few of us know much about their bodies. If I asked how many legs they had, you might not know the answer but I reckon not everyone will even know they had legs. Did you know they had their stomach in their head? Or that this little group of marine invertebrates were some of the first animals ever to develop not only complex eyes but also a sophisticated visual system.

Starting with the basics, trilobites ranged in size from just 3–4mm long to over 45cm, and weighed as much as 4.5kg, the equivalent of more than four bags of sugar. One spectacular fossil found in Canada measured a whopping 72cm from end to end.

1.5m

4mm

45cm

72cm

The name trilobite tells us they were made up of three sections (or lobes). Although it's really tempting to think these sections are easy to identify and are the 'head' section, the 'body' section and the 'tail' section, they are instead named for the lobes running along the body, from the front to the back. There is a lobe down the centre of the body, a second on the left side and a third on the right side of the body. There are, however, still other clearly separated sections:

The pygidium (pi-jid-EE-um), which was the 'tail' end and made up from a number of segments fused together.

The thorax (thor-ax), made up from, usually, 10-12 sections, all linked together.

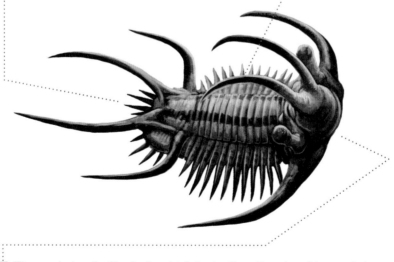

The cephalon (seff-a-lon), which is the 'head' end and housed the eyes, antennae, mouthparts and, weirdly, the animal's stomach...

How often have you seen a trilobite fossil? Lots? How often have you seen the top of the animal and how often have you actually seen its *underside*? I was pretty old the first time I ever saw what was actually underneath that protective exoskeleton and it was this that gave me my fascination and appreciation for these wonderful and complex little marine organisms. The reason we rarely get a glimpse underneath the shell is either because the animal died in a way which preserved its upper side or because a lot of what was underneath the outer shell was either delicate (like the antennae) or was what we call 'soft tissue', such as a digestive system, which rarely fossilises.

Some very well-preserved specimens have been discovered, though, and scientists have been able to scan them with X-rays. Using the knowledge we have from living arthropods (arrth-RO pod) – invertebrate animals with an exoskeleton – it's possible to have a better understanding of what the inside of a trilobite might have looked like. The big, round, bulging head section actually contained the stomach, meaning a lot of digestion took place directly behind the mouthparts. It is thought that those species with an especially rounded cephalon were

Having a hard exoskeleton meant that trilobites needed to shed their tough exterior at intervals throughout their lives. This allowed them to both grow and be safe from predators.

often predatory and used their bulging 'head-stomach' to store larger prey items (or pieces of their unlucky prey).

At the opposite end of the body was an anus and between this and the 'head' would have been a long digestive 'tube'. Running down the length of the body would have been the heart and, unlike us and other vertebrates, trilobites did not have blood. Like other arthropods, they had a liquid similar to blood called haemolymph (HE-MO limp-ff). This did not run through arteries, veins and capillaries but just washed through the inside of their body in what we call an 'open' system. Gills were used to filter oxygen from the water and ran in little mat-like structures between their legs and the underside of the exoskeleton and their legs. Along their legs ran spiny structures called gnathobases (nay-THO bay-sez) which helped them break up their food.

Some trilobites were predators, while others fell victim to predators themselves. Although they had a protective hard exoskeleton which would have acted like a suit of armour, most could also roll into a protective ball, making it much harder for predators to eat them. Controlled by muscles, the flexible pieces of shell which connected the harder exoskeleton bent and pulled the animal into a defensive ball, where in some species the different parts of the exoskeleton even locked together tightly. In a species with spines along its exoskeleton, these would have made this defensive behaviour even more effective.

Although an exoskeleton is protective, having a hard shell covering the outside of the body meant trilobites could not grow continuously throughout their lifetime. Instead, like all invertebrates with an exoskeleton, they shed their hardened shell at intervals in order to grow. This would have been an especially vulnerable time for these animals, as they needed to pump water into their new exoskeleton to make it harder and able to defend them from attack. As they started to moult each time, their exoskeleton would first split along the cephalon, creating a little hatch. To help the process, the trilobite arched its body and, if it had any spines, would have anchored them in the sand or between rocks to give it some extra support.

Imagine you grew up always wearing gloves, but the only way your hands would ever get any bigger was to pull the gloves off every so often and replace them with larger ones. This is similar (but only a little bit) to what happens when an arthropod moults from its exoskeleton.

To protect themselves from hungry predators, such as this armoured *Ptyctodus*, trilobites were able to roll into defensive balls.

One of the most impressive features of trilobites is their eyes. They weren't the first animals to develop eyes, but they were one of the first groups to possess an impressive and complex visual system.

Unlike our eyes, which have a single lens, trilobites had eyes with a wide variation in the number of lenses on each eye, ranging from one to 15,000. Eyes with lots of lenses like this are known as compound eyes. It is thought that a major benefit of compound eyes is that they are effective at detecting movement, such as an approaching predator. They were also the first type of vision system which could actually detect the direction of things. Whereas before, an animal might be able to sense light or dark, having compound eyes meant they could detect where the light was actually coming from.

This was an important and significant step in the evolution of vision in the animal kingdom. But it wasn't perfect. If you do a little experiment for me,

you can demonstrate how impressive your eyes are. Have a look at the words on this page first of all. Now, have a look at something far away, such as a bird flying or a mountain in the distance, or even the moon, if you're awake quite late. When you move between looking at something next to you and then far away, the lens in your eye changes shape to focus according to the distance of the object. But trilobites had lots (or even thousands) of lenses in each eye and these lenses were not able to change shape. This meant they could only focus on things close by *or* far away, but not both. This would have risked them missing opportunities to hunt or avoid being hunted.

But trilobites had an extra trick up their evolutionary sleeves. Rather than having just one layer of lenses, they had two, which focused in slightly different ways. This was an incredibly successful adaptation and the combination of the two layers meant they could focus on things close by *and* further away.

CLASSIFICATION 🧩🧩

You might think that because the trilobites were such a successful group for so long and because they left many fossils from different species that we'd have a good idea about what a trilobite actually *was* and what they were related to. But it's not quite as simple as that. We don't know as much as you might expect about their evolution, such as how they were related to other animals or even how we should think of them in terms of describing what *sort* of animal a trilobite actually was.

They were early members of the arthropods, a group of invertebrates that have a hard exoskeleton and segmented legs. Today, insects (such as dragonflies and ants), arachnids (such as mites and spiders) and crustaceans (such as crabs and woodlice) are all examples of living (or extant) arthropods. Back in the

Permian and the periods directly before it, trilobites represented the arthropods long before the insects, arachnids or crustaceans had evolved.

Within the arthropods, they sit in their own group, called the Trilobita. There are so many species of trilobites recorded that scientists believe they are the most diverse group of extinct animals that have been identified so far. For example, we know of between 1,000 and 1,500 species of extinct dinosaurs, whereas around 20,000 species of trilobites have been discovered and described already, with more being found every year.

Investigating a family tree can be difficult. When I looked into my own past, I found that because documents were either lost or not filled out properly hundreds of years ago, or because there were lots of people with similar names, it's not easy to trace your ancestry back as far as you might like. I think I can get as far as about 1740 (and I'm really happy with that). It does mean that there will be people walking around who are part of my family but I have never met. I may even have bumped into some of them, but it would now be almost impossible to know how we are related.

Imagine if I tried to trace my family tree back a thousand years. Or a million years. Or more. This is the issue with trilobites. It is so far back that it's difficult to be certain about what they evolved from and what they are most closely related to in animals alive today.

For a time, trilobites sat with the crustaceans, but this changed, as palaeontologists and other scientists understood more and more about them, and then placed them alongside the arachnids. However, as we learned even more, it was decided that because their bodies were separated into three sections they were different enough from every other group to have earned their own, the Trilobita – a separate but extinct group of arthropods containing trilobites and some of their closest relatives.

The lack of a complete picture of trilobite classification and the ever-increasing understanding of how we see them is a wonderful example of how science really works and what it means to be a scientist. It's easy to think that because it's straightforward to identify something and because it's familiar to us, that we should know a lot, if not everything, about it. But as more evidence is discovered all the time, new techniques and equipment become available, and more scientists work together around the world, our knowledge and understanding evolves as much as any group of animals.

ECOLOGY 🦐

Every species has its own ecology, which means the relationship that species has with other species and the interactions it has with its environment. Looking at a species on its own never gives you the full picture. I have spent a lot of time with different wild animals around the world and each has a different ecology.

Imagine a polar bear. Did you think of a big white bear on its own, or did you picture its ecology? When I think of a beautiful polar bear, I see one walking along a dark strip of stony shoreline, stepping around the clumps of tough Arctic grasses, her cub running beside her. There are thick sheets of ice in the shallow cold waters next to her and the land above her is white with snow. At the end of the bay in front of them is a group of bearded seals, enjoying the morning sun. They haven't spotted her yet. Flying high above is a single ivory gull which has followed her for days, hoping to scavenge a meal if she makes a kill.

OK, this is a bit of a full mental picture, but for me, it's just natural to imagine the ecology of an organism. What do *you* see when you imagine a tarantula, or what is a vulture doing when you picture it?

To understand as much as we can about an organism, we need to think about its ecology, which includes its physical habitat and all the other types of organism that share its environment.

Looking at the ecology of the trilobites is not an easy task because they were so successful. In my example, it would be unusual to think of a polar bear in the desert or wading through the shallow waters of a tropical coral reef. I'd assume you'd think about a polar ecology, and more specifically a northern one, so no penguins or leopard seals in sight. But what happens when you imagine an ant? Is it in your garden or in the cracks in the pavement of your local street cleaning up scraps of food? Or is it living among the thorns of an acacia tree in Africa, defending it against giraffes and other herbivores? Maybe your ant is in the Australian outback, with kangaroos bouncing overhead, or in the Brazilian rainforest, cutting up sections of leaves to take back to its nest so it can farm fungi to eat. Ants are everywhere and are so successful that they have an almost limitless number of ecologies.

The same was pretty much true for trilobites. They inhabited a broad range of marine ecosystems, from deep to shallow environments; they were found both in the open ocean and along shorelines, and in cold waters as much as in warm waters. There is also some evidence to suggest some were able to actually crawl out of the sea and on to the shore, maybe to feed. Because they also sat at so many positions within marine food chains and food webs, from being both predators to prey and from filter feeders to scavengers, their ecology was not only complex but a crucial part of almost every marine environment for over 250 million years.

Trilobites may not have been the most scary-looking animals or the largest or even the most active marine inhabitants, but nevertheless, they were an essential part of the success for the ecology in ancient oceans. It appears that without trilobites, there may not have been sea scorpions, unusually shaped sharks such as *Helicoprion* (hel-EE cop ree on) or even the mighty *Dunkleosteus*.

In the oceans, any big dead animal is an opportunity and a decaying giant shark such as *Helicoprion* would have fed scavengers for months, if not years.

When

The first trilobites appeared in the fossil record during the Cambrian period, about 530 million years ago. They thrived throughout the Palaeozoic era, until the Late Devonian mass extinction 161 million years later, where many groups went extinct at the same time as *Dunkleosteus*. By the start of the Permian period, only one group of trilobites was left.

The Proetida (PRO-TEE da) was a big group with lots of different species, but the true diversity of the trilobites never really recovered after the Devonian period. They finally went extinct at the end of the Permian period, 252 million years ago, bringing their quarter of a billion year-long story on Earth to a close.

Where

Trilobites remain one of the most widespread marine fossils and can be found in sediment from shallow and deep marine environments, as well as in deep sea and shallow coastal habitats and from warm- and cold-water areas. It is safe to say that they had a global distribution and would have been at home in any marine ecosystem.

This is how the Earth looked at the end of the Permian period.

Environment 🌍

The Permian period lasted for a little under 50 million years and during that time, conditions on the planet changed from a global ice age at the start of the Permian to being much warmer by the end. As the ice melted, the middle of the huge continental land mass dried out. Land changed from the supercontinent called Pangaea (pan JEE-a) at the start of the period, breaking up into smaller (yet still very large) continental land masses as time passed.

As the land began to break up, it created a massive shallow ocean. Previously, the super-ocean Panthalassa (pan-tha lass-a) had been the only marine environment, but by the end of the Permian, the Palaeo-Tethys (PAY-LEE-O teth-izz) Ocean had formed, which would later lead to the creation of the Tethys Ocean. These large oceans surrounded by land would have influenced the climate and would have created monsoon conditions where seasons of heavy rainfall were common. Further inland it would have been much hotter and drier and much of Pangaea would have been desert.

When we take a look at the average environmental conditions across the 46 or so million years which made up the Permian period, we see that the concentration of carbon dioxide was roughly three times higher than it is now all the way through the Permian, despite the massive rise around the mass extinction. The average surface temperature on Earth was 16°C, which is 1°C more than the average surface temperature now. This increase may not sound like much but it makes a huge difference. Even the sea level was different then, ranging from 60m higher than we see today, to 20m lower than current levels, depending on whether the Earth was experiencing a warmer or cooler phase.

Understanding evolution can help us explore relationships between ourselves and extinct animals such as the huge *Dimetrodon*, seen here basking in the sun, with a colourful *Varanops* resting on her snout.

Flora and fauna 🌿🐟

As a group, trilobites were around for hundreds of millions of years and they would have seen extensive changes in their world. One of these changes would have been the other animals and plants evolving around them. Any marine invertebrate is always going to end up on the dinner menu of another oceanic inhabitant, even if they are an invertebrate too. For most of the time that trilobites trundled and swam through the Earth's prehistoric oceans, their main worry in life seems to have been either the early arthropod predator *Anomalocaris* or later, the giant eurypterid 'sea scorpion'.

Both these marine
predators would have
hunted smaller trilobites
but as some eurypterids grew
to over 2.5m in length, even
larger species might have ended up
as a meal.

Even the giant predatory fish
Dunkleosteus may have snacked on larger,
free-swimming trilobites

during the Devonian
period, and although
we don't yet know
whether the 12m-
long *Helicoprion*,

with its unique whorl
of deadly teeth, was a
trilobite predator or not, these
huge sharks would definitely have
shared the trilobites' environment
during the early Permian
period.

Like oceans now, prehistoric marine ecosystems were thriving but inhabited by organisms unrecognisable today. Here, pelagic trilobites swim by giant cephalopods such as *Endoceras*, ancient relatives of octopus and squid.

The Earth during the Permian period looked a very different place, both beneath and above the waves. On land, terrestrial environments were dominated by two groups throughout the Permian period: the sauropsids (sor-op sidz), which means 'lizard face' and now includes the reptiles and birds, and the synapsids (sin ap-sidz), a group containing the mammals and our ancestors.

During the Permian, however, different animals made up the group. Early synapsids were sometimes called mammal-like reptiles, because in the past we treated them as something between mammals and reptiles, but scientists dropped this term, as they were not in fact mammals. Instead, we call these early synapsids the 'proto-mammals'.

There was a wide and strange range of early synapsids, including my two favourite prehistoric animals. One of the largest of the early terrestrial predators was *Dimetrodon*, a four-legged predator with a jaw full of different-sized teeth, a long, powerful tail and, most famously, a large sail made from the long bony spines of the vertebrae along its back. With some species of *Dimetrodon* reaching more than 4m in length, they would have dominated many of the early Permian food chains.

Throughout the Permian, as with every period of Earth's history, species evolved and species went extinct regardless of mass extinctions. Around eight million years after *Dimetrodon* went extinct, the small-headed, large-bodied *Moschops* appeared. These large herbivores may have lived a semi-aquatic life, like a very early hippopotamus, and possibly used their round, thick skulls to headbutt each other in fights to establish dominance and defend territories. Both *Dimetrodon* and *Moschops* had gone extinct millions of years before the End Permian mass extinction occurred.

It was during the Permian that some of the first trees we still see today appeared, and from the fossil record, scientists are able to identify ginkgo trees and some very early evergreen conifers. Ferns and the palm-like cycads, which are still around today and look like a tree trunk with a cross between fern and palm leaves sprouting from the top, were also commonly found throughout this time.

After displaying, two large *Moschops* fight for territory, while an *Alopecognathus*, a predatory therapsid (a group including the mammals and our extinct relatives), observes from the safety of a tree.

Behaviour

Don't forget, fossils were once living, breathing organisms and, more than that, they actually *did* stuff. It's easy to imagine the behaviour of larger animals like sabre-toothed cats hunting their prey, or sauropod dinosaurs moving across the land in vast herds, but it's more difficult when we look at the fossils from smaller animals, and those animals were invertebrates.

I admit that even I find this with trilobites sometimes. I don't know about you, but when I think about a trilobite, my mind goes to a fossil shop or a museum. I visualise a little stone animal, locked in time in that familiar trilobite shape. I find it hard to imagine a living trilobite doing anything. But trilobites were a fascinating group of animals, and showed a wide range of shapes, sizes and behaviours.

First of allow, how do we *know* different species of trilobites showed a range of different behaviours? Scientists are experts at following clues and looking at the evidence, and when lots of similar animals are found together in the same place at the same time, there are only two possible explanations. Either they all act the same and there is a huge amount of competition between them, which isn't a great idea, or they have slight differences, maybe in the way they move, how they eat, *what* they eat, or even when they are awake or asleep.

African cats are a good example of this. There are quite a few species of cat in Africa, and many of them share the same habitat, but slight differences between them mean they can live in the same place at the same time. They can coexist. Lions are very big, hunt in prides and are able to take down prey as large as elephants. Leopards usually live and hunt alone and take down smaller prey, but then drag it up a tree to eat in safety. Cheetahs are the fastest-running animals on the planet and chase down prey that leopards and lions often can't catch.

Then there are the spectacular caracals, which are able to jump high into the air, making them formidable predators of birds, while servals are experts at hunting rodents, hares and even frogs. These are all cats and all predators, but because of their differences, they reduce or remove the problem of competition and they're able to take advantage of the same environment.

The same seems to have been the case for trilobites. Often thousands (or even more) are found fossilised with different species preserved together. At a location in Wales,

Although it is tempting to think that trilobite fossils look quite similar, the group included predators and prey, scavengers and filter feeders. Some lived on the seabed, while others swam freely. The prehistoric Welsh coastline was especially rich in trilobites.

for example, 11 different trilobite species can be found together in the same rock. This may not sound like very many, seeing as there were over 20,000 species in total, but 11 species from the same location at the same time is pretty impressive.

We can strengthen the idea that different species were doing different things by looking at some exceptionally well-preserved trilobite fossils, which *actually* show us how they moved, and even how and what they ate. From such fossils, we can tell that there was a big split between the open-water, swimming trilobite species, which are known as being pelagic (pell-aj ik), and those which scurried and moved around on the seabed, meaning

they were benthic (ben-th ik) animals. Within the pelagic and benthic habitats of the same marine environment, some of these little animals were scavengers, while others were filter feeders. Some were even predators and hunted other marine invertebrates. Finally, even the different sizes of the species meant they would have eaten different things and this would have helped keep competition as low as possible. The largest Welsh trilobites, for example, were over 10 times the size of the smallest, which were just 3 or 4mm long.

Like marine invertebrates today, trilobites filled many levels of the food chain, from filter feeders and scavengers to predators. Here, a spiny trilobite from the Devonian period pulls a marine worm out from the sediment.

If you were suddenly transported back to the time when trilobites were alive and you were dropped somewhere in one of the vast marine habitats which dominated our planet then, you'd have a good chance of seeing a trilobite during your prehistoric snorkelling adventure. This is because they were found in deep waters and shallow coastal habitats, cold polar waters and warm tropical reefs and they ate a wide range of food. The majority of trilobite species appear to have been scavengers and predators, hunting soft-bodied prey such as marine worms, wherever they could.

Unlike marine invertebrate predators and scavengers alive today, trilobites did not have all the 'mouthparts' at the head end of the body. Instead, they had a mouth, as you might expect, but it was along the edges of the underside of their body, and they also had rows of spiny structures called gnathobases, which were used to crush food and tear prey into smaller pieces. It's a little bit like you having teeth in your armpits! Once food was broken into bite-sized chunks, it was transported up to the mouth, where it was eaten. Some crustaceans alive today, such as the fascinating horseshoe crabs, also have these structures and prepare their meals in a similar way to trilobites.

There were also filter-feeding trilobites and others with large eyes and streamlined bodies, which swam through the water and hunted zooplankton, the wide variety of small young and adult animals which have lived drifting in our oceans for millions of years.

Trilobites are one of those animals we are used to associating with prehistoric marine environments and seeing in artistic recreations of these ancient places, but at the same time, they are a group that often goes unappreciated. The largest species grew up to 250 times the size of the smallest, and they filled every part of the environment, whether as fast, active predators or slow-moving filter feeders. They were found in every area of every ocean and were a part of marine aquatic life for hundreds of millions of years. They survived at least two mass extinctions and it took the worst natural disaster in the history of our planet, the Great Dying, to finally make these ultimate animals go extinct.

GLOSSARY

Anoxia (an ox-EE-a)
When the levels of oxygen drop low, to dangerous levels.

Apex (AY-pex) predator
When a predator sits at the very top of a food chain and has no natural predators.

Arthropod (arrth-RO pod)
An invertebrate animal with an exoskeleton and segmented pairs of legs. Insects, such as beetles; arachnids, such as spiders; and crustaceans, such as crabs, are all examples of arthropods.

Benthic (ben-th ik)
The lowest level of an aquatic ecosystem. It might be a stream bed and the water just above it, or the bottom of the ocean, with the seabed and water just above it being the benthic zone.

Ecology

The particular area of biology where the focus is on the relationship between organisms and their surroundings.

Environment (en-vire-on ment)

The 'surroundings' in which an organism, or a group of organisms, lives. This includes other species as well as weather, climate, mountains, deserts, rivers, lakes, oceans, and so on.

Equator (EE-KWAY tor)

This imaginary line runs around the centre of the Earth and passes through the tropics. It is halfway between the North and South poles and is also known as zero degrees latitude.

Exoskeleton

A rigid external covering for the body in some invertebrate animals, especially arthropods.

Fauna (for-naa)

The animals found in a particular place or from a particular time.

Gigatonne

A way to measure the force of an explosion. One gigatonne is the same as one trillion kilograms, about the weight of a trillion bags of sugar, or the same force as one billion sticks of dynamite exploding at the same time.

Gnathobases (nay-THO bay-sez)

The thin, spiny structures found running along the legs of trilobites which they used to help break up their food.

Greenhouse gas

Like an actual greenhouse, greenhouse gases are able to trap heat. They prevent the trapped heat from escaping through our atmosphere. Carbon dioxide is a greenhouse gas. We need greenhouse gases to keep our planet warm enough for life to exist but if their levels get too high, we start seeing environmental problems through global warming.

Organism (or-gan IZ-mm)

Any living thing. A tree is an organism, so is a shark, and a mushroom. You are an organism.

Ozone

A gas naturally found in high concentrations above the Earth. Ozone blocks much of the ultraviolet (UV) energy from the sun from hitting the planet.

Pangaea (pan JEE-a)

A supercontinent from around 335 million years ago, made up of the modern land masses which back then sat together. Pangaea started to break up through the movement of tectonic plates around 175 million years ago.

Pelagic (pell-aj ik)
The open ocean zone zone. Pelagic describes species that live in the open sea, not in waters close to land or inland.

Sauropsids (sor-op sidz)
A group of land-living vertebrates which includes all the existing reptiles and birds, and their extinct ancestors.

Supercontinent (SOO-per con-tin-ent)
At times throughout the history of the Earth, all the available land on the planet has been one big mass of land. This is a supercontinent.

Synapsids (sin ap-sidz)
A group of vertebrate animals that includes mammals and all the extinct animals more closely related to mammals than to any other group.

Tectonic (tek-ton-ik)
Relating to the structure of the Earth's crust and the processes which occur within it.

Terrestrial (terr-ess TREE-all)
On the land.

Zooplankton
The tiny animal organisms found in marine and some freshwater ecosystems.

Collect all eight titles
in the EXTINCT *series*

 Hallucigenia

 Dunkleosteus

 *Trilobite*

Lisowicia

 *Tyrannosaurus rex*

 *Megalodon*

 *Thylacine*

 *Hainan gibbon*

THE STORY OF LIFE ON EARTH

EXTINCT

HALLUCIGENIA

SUPER-WEIRD

BEN GARROD

ILLUSTRATED BY **GABRIEL UGUETO**

One of the oldest and most mysterious animals ever described, *Hallucigenia* was a kind of sea-living armoured worm. But it was nothing like the worms we know today. Its body was covered in spines and frills. It had claws at the end of its legs and a mouth lined with sharp teeth.

This strange animal was one of the victims of the End Ordovician mass extinction which claimed 85 per cent of the species living in the world's oceans around 443 million years ago. What could have led to this catastrophe and what caused the appearance of huge glaciers and falling sea levels, leaving many marine ecosystems dry and unable to sustain life at a time when it had only just got started?

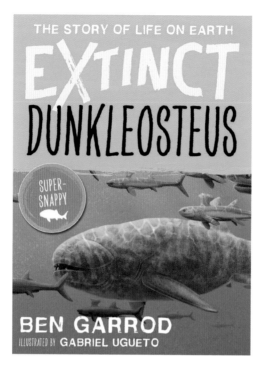

THE STORY OF LIFE ON EARTH
EXTINCT
DUNKLEOSTEUS

SUPER-
SNAPPY

BEN GARROD
ILLUSTRATED BY **GABRIEL UGUETO**

An armoured fish with a bite 10 times more powerful than that of a great white shark, *Dunkleosteus* could also snap its jaws five times faster than you can blink! It was one of the most iconic predators ever to rule the waves. What was it like to live in its shadow? And how did it become one of the many victims of the Late Devonian mass extinction around 375 million years ago?

Let's discover why this mass extinction only affected ocean life and why it went on for so long – some scientists believe it lasted for 25 million years. In a weird twist, we'll look at whether the evolution of trees on the land at that time was partly responsible for the loss of so many marine species, including *Dunkleosteus*.

THE STORY OF LIFE ON EARTH

E✕TINCT

LISOWICIA

SUPER-SIZED

BEN GARROD

ILLUSTRATED BY GABRIEL UGUETO

At a massive 9 tonnes, the elephant-sized *Lisowicia* was one of the largest animals on the planet during the Late Triassic. A kind of cross between a mammal and a reptile but not quite either, *Lisowicia* was a distant cousin of the ancient mammals – and they eventually led to our very own ancestors.

We'll discover why the End Triassic mass extinction happened, changing the global environment and making life impossible for around 75 per cent of species. And how, while this fourth mass extinction may have been devastating for most life on Earth, it gave one group of animals – dinosaurs – the chance to dominate the planet for millions of years.

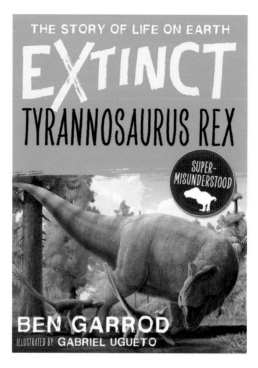

THE STORY OF LIFE ON EARTH

EXTINCT

TYRANNOSAURUS REX

SUPER-MISUNDERSTOOD

BEN GARROD

ILLUSTRATED BY **GABRIEL UGUETO**

Weighing as much as three adult elephants and as long as a bus, *Tyrannosaurus rex* was one of the mightiest land predators that has ever lived. It had the most powerful bite of any dinosaur and dominated its environment. But not even the biggest dinosaurs were a match for what happened at the end of the Cretaceous, about 66 million years ago.

What happened when an asteroid travelling at almost 40,000km/h crashed into Earth? Creating a shockwave that literally shook the world, its impact threw millions of tonnes of red-hot ash and dust into the atmosphere, blocking out the sun and destroying 75 per cent of life on Earth. Any living thing bigger than a fox was gone and this fifth global mass extinction meant the end of the dinosaurs as we knew them.

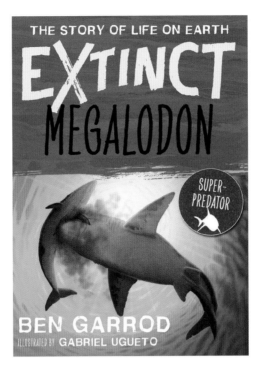

THE STORY OF LIFE ON EARTH

EXTINCT
MEGALODON

SUPER-PREDATOR

BEN GARROD

ILLUSTRATED BY **GABRIEL UGUETO**

A giant marine predator, megalodon grew up to an incredible 18m – longer than three great white sharks, nose to tail. This ferocious monster had the most powerful bite force ever measured. It specialised in killing whales by attacking them from the side, aiming for their heart and lungs.

But, like more than 50 per cent of marine mammals and many others, megalodon disappeared in the End Pliocene mass extinction around 2.5 million years ago. We'll find out why this event affected many of the bigger animals in the marine environment and had an especially bad impact on both warm-blooded animals and predators.

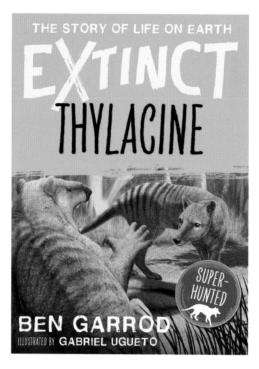

THE STORY OF LIFE ON EARTH

EXTINCT
THYLACINE

SUPER-HUNTED

BEN GARROD

ILLUSTRATED BY **GABRIEL UGUETO**

The thylacine, also known as the Tasmanian tiger, is one of a long list of species, ranging from sabre-toothed cats to the dodo, that have been wiped out by humans. The last wild thylacine was shot in 1930 and the last captive thylacine alive died in a zoo in 1936.

We'll explore the mass extinction we are now entering and how we, as a species, have the power to wipe out other species – something no other single species is able to do. Who are the winners and losers and why might it take over seven million years to restore mammal diversity on Earth to what it was before humans arrived?

THE STORY OF LIFE ON EARTH
EXTINCT
HAINAN GIBBON
SUPER-SURVIVOR?
BEN GARROD
ILLUSTRATED BY GABRIEL UGUETO

One of the most endangered animals on our planet, the Hainan gibbon is also one of our closest living relatives. Family groups of these little primates live in the trees on an island off the south coast of China and they feed on leaves and fruit.

But the gibbons are now in serious trouble because of the effects of human population increase around the world and habitat destruction. Without action, this animal might soon be extinct and need a dagger after its name. What can we all do to help stop some of our most interesting, iconic and important species from going extinct?

BEN GARROD is Professor of Evolutionary Biology and Science Engagement at the University of East Anglia. Ben has lived and worked all around the world, alongside chimpanzees in Africa, polar bears in the Arctic and giant dinosaur fossils in South America. He is currently based in the West Country. He broadcasts regularly on TV and radio and is trustee and ambassador of a number of key conservation organisations. His debut six-book series *So You Think You Know About... Dinosaurs?* and *The Chimpanzee and Me* are also published by Zephyr.

GABRIEL UGUETO is a scientific illustrator, palaeoartist and herpetologist based in Florida. For several years, he was an independent herpetologist researcher and authored papers on new species of neotropical lizards and various taxonomic revisions. As an illustrator, his work reflects the latest scientific hypotheses about the external appearance and the behaviour of the animals, both extinct and extant, that he reconstructs. His illustrations have appeared in books, journals, magazines, museum exhibitions and television documentaries.

Zephyr is an imprint of Head of Zeus.
At Zephyr we are proud to publish books
you can read and re-read time and time
again because they tell a brilliant story
and because they entertain you.

 @_ZephyrBooks

 @_zephyrbooks

 HeadofZeusBooks

readzephyr.com

www.headofzeus.com

ZEPHYR